Management: Danny Goldberg and Ron Stone
Gold Mountain Entertainment
Production Manager: Daniel Rosenbaum
Art Direction: Alisa Hill
Administration: Marianne Monroe
Director of Music: Mark Phillips

ISBN: 0-89524-502-7

Edited by Milton Okun

CONTENTS

LOVE IS A BATTLEFIELD

Words and Music by Holly Knight
and Mike Chapman

5

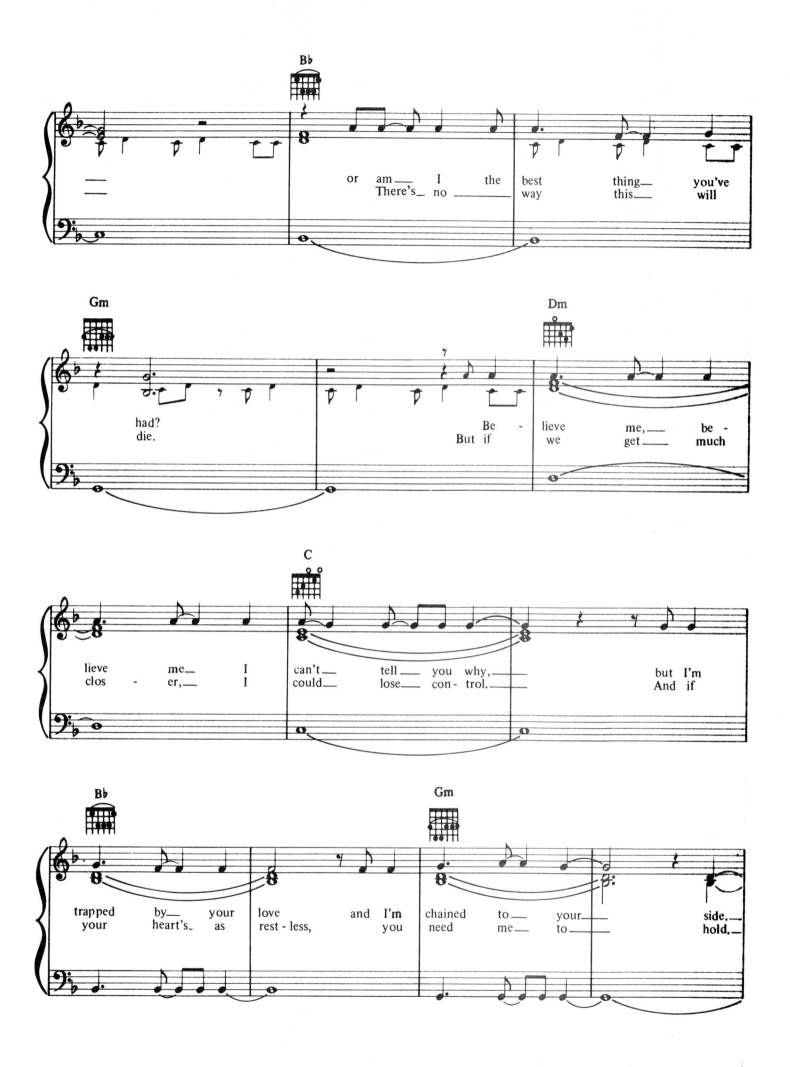

HIT ME WITH YOUR BEST SHOT

Words and Music by Eddie Schwartz

11

come on with a come on, you don't fight fair,— But that's O. K.

see if I___ care!___ Knock me down it's all___ in vain;___ I'll

get right back on my feet a - gain.___

D.S. al Coda

Coda

HELL IS FOR CHILDREN

**Words and Music by Neil Geraldo,
Pat Benatar and Roger Capps**

They

17

Love and pain __ be - come one __ and the same __ in the eyes __

__ of a wound - ed child, __ be - cause hell,

hell is for chil - dren,

and you know __ that their lit - tle lives __

It's all so con-fus-ing this bru-tal a-bus-ing,

They black-en your eyes and

SHADOWS OF THE NIGHT

Words and Music by D.L. Byron

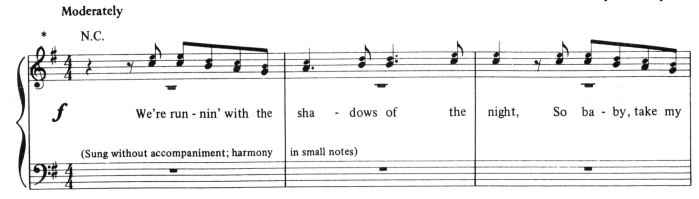

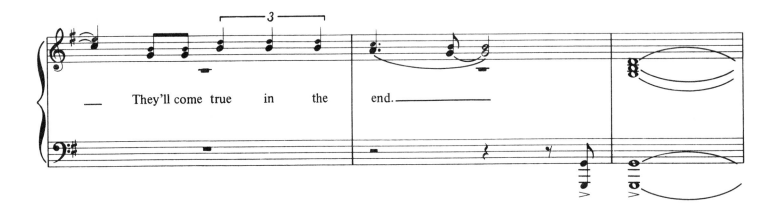

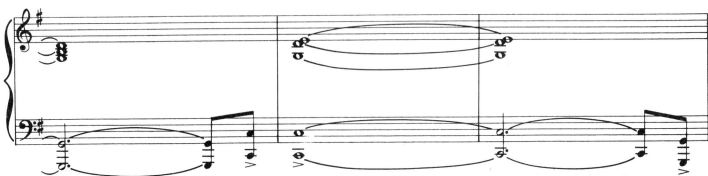

* Recorded ½ step lower in G♭ major; to play with record mentally change key signature to 6 flats and play written notes.

*2nd time, play bass in ♩ ♪ ♪ ♪ ↘ rhythm

And now the hands of time are stand-ing still____

ALL FIRED UP

Words and Music by Kerryn Tolhurst,
Myron Grombacher and Pat Giraldo

All — fi - red up. All fi - red up.

Now, I — be - lieve — there comes — a time — when ev - 'ry - thing — just falls —

All — fi - red up.

All — fi - red up, fi - red up, fi - red

— in line. — We live — an' learn — from our — mis - takes. —

up.

Ain't no - bod -y

INVINCIBLE
(THEME FROM "THE LEGEND OF BILLIE JEAN")

Words and Music by Holly Knight
and Simon Climie

*Instrumental omitted.

WE BELONG

Words and Music by D.E. Lowen
and D. Navarro

to the doubts that com - pli - cate___ your mind.___ We be - long to the
Now there's no turn - ing back.___ When you say we be - long to the
I see your face ev - 'ry - where.___ Still you say we be - long to the

light; we be - long to the thun - der.
light, we be - long to the thun - der.
light; we be - long to the thun - der.

We be -

long to the sound of the words we've both fall - en un - der.

What - ev - er we de - ny or em - brace for worse or for

46

HEARTBREAKER

Words and Music by Cliff Wade
and Geoff Gill

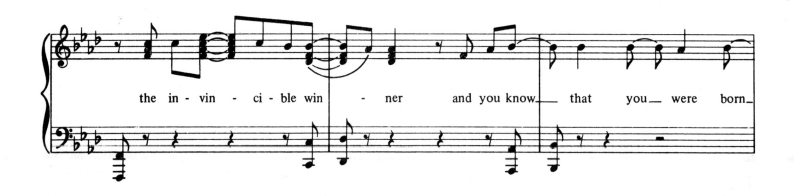

the in - vin - ci - ble win - ner and you know ___ that you ___ were born ___

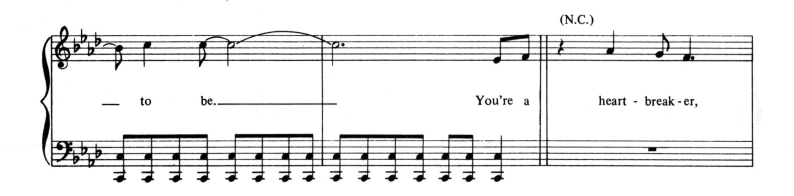

(N.C.)

___ to be. ___ You're a heart - break - er,

dream mak - er, love tak - er, don't you mess a - round with me! You're a

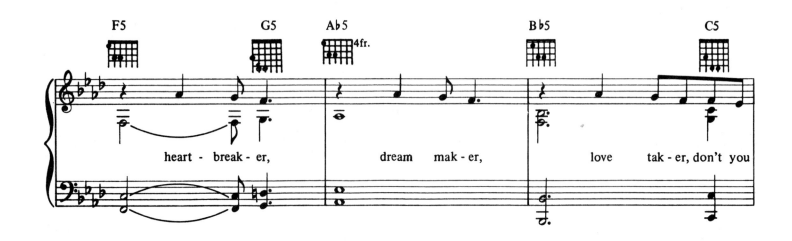

F5   G5   Ab5 4fr.   Bb5   C5

heart - break - er, dream mak - er, love tak - er, don't you

ONE LOVE

Words and Music by Neil Geraldo
and Myron Grombacher

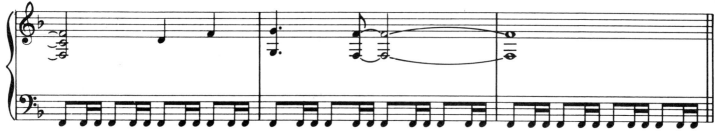

Once there was__ a man_____ and he lived to sing the li - on's song__
Once there was__ a man_____ and his words be - came a song of love,__
Hear the li - on's song,_____ voic - es cry - in' like a des - ert wind__

as he trav - eled on the road of hope.__
and his song be - came the gold - en dream.__
Yeah, he's gone un - to his fa - ther's land.__

One love is— the light_____ shin - ing o - ver ev - 'ry moun - tain - top._
One love is— the light_____ shin - ing o - ver ev - 'ry - one that be - lieves.
Af - ri - ka to - night,_____ for we tru - ly are one in our hearts._

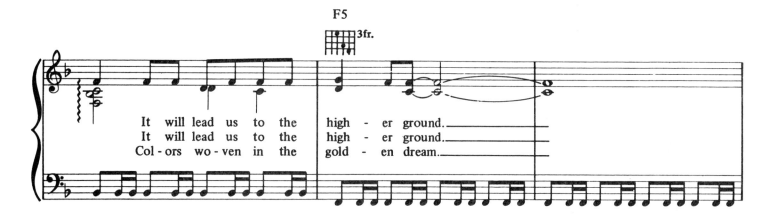

It will lead us to the high - er ground._
It will lead us to the high - er ground._
Col - ors wo - ven in the gold - en dream._

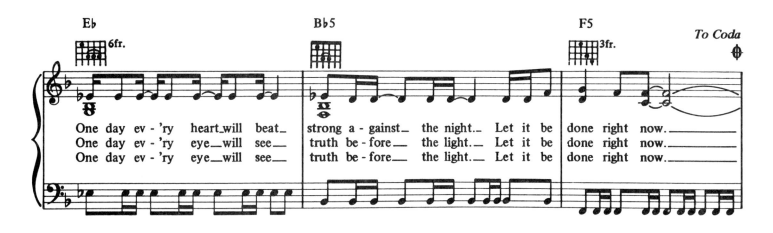

One day ev - 'ry heart_will beat_ strong a - gainst_ the night.. Let it be done right now.____
One day ev - 'ry eye_will see_ truth be - fore_ the light._ Let it be done right now.____
One day ev - 'ry eye_will see_ truth be - fore_ the light._ Let it be done right now.____

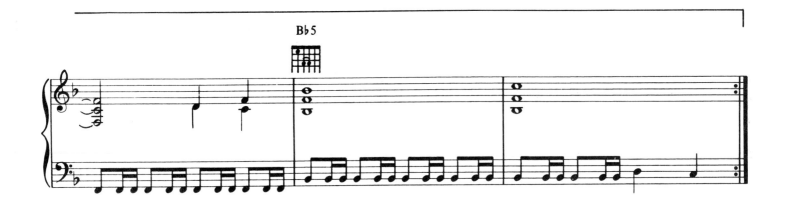

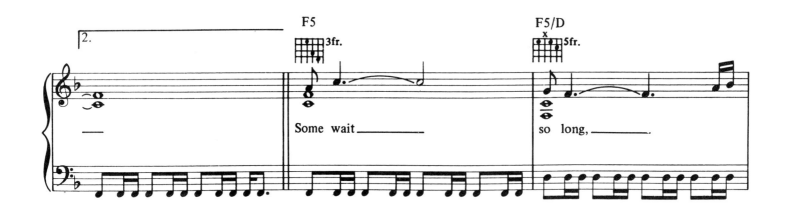

trav-eled on _____ will lead us home for-ev-

er. _____

D.S. al Coda Coda

One day ev-'ry voice_will speak_ strong a-gainst_ the night._ Let us be one right now. _____

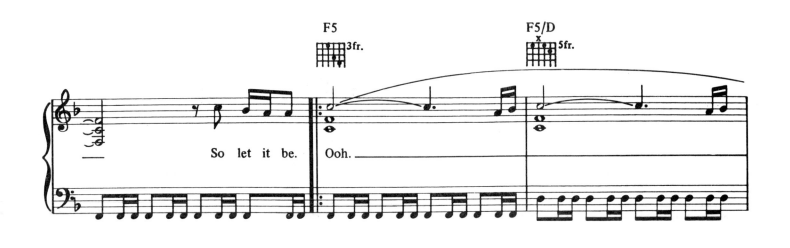

So let it be. Ooh._____

Ooh.

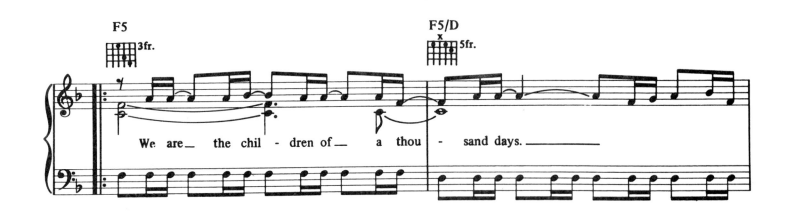

We are__ the chil - dren of__ a thou - sand days._____

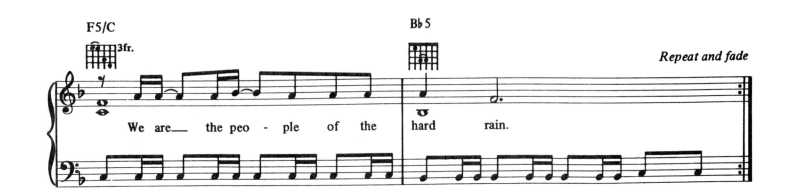

Repeat and fade

We are__ the peo - ple of the hard rain.

WE LIVE FOR LOVE

Straight - ahead rock ($\stackrel{\text{.}}{\text{.}}$ = 136)

Words and Music by Neil Geraldo

Your love's con - ta - gious,_____
When we get tired_____

one kiss is dan -
and watch the sum -

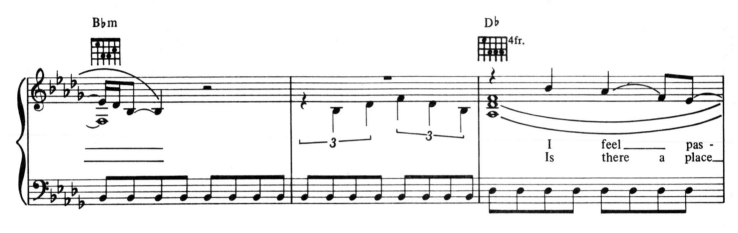

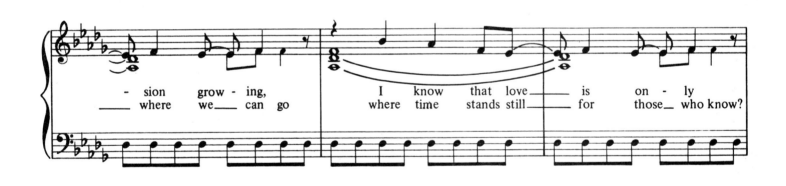

FIRE AND ICE

Words and Music by Tom Kelly,
Scott Sheets and Pat Benatar

You'll just tear it a - part.

So you think you got it all fig - ured out, you're an ex - pert in the field with - out a doubt.

But I know your meth - ods in - side and out and I won't be tak - en in

by   fire _____ and ice.

PROMISES IN THE DARK

Words and Music by Neil Geraldo
and Pat Benatar

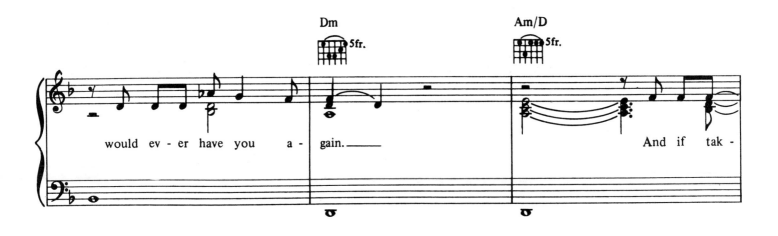

would ev - er have you a - gain.____ And if tak -

- in' was gon - na get done____ you'd de - cide__ where and when. Just when you

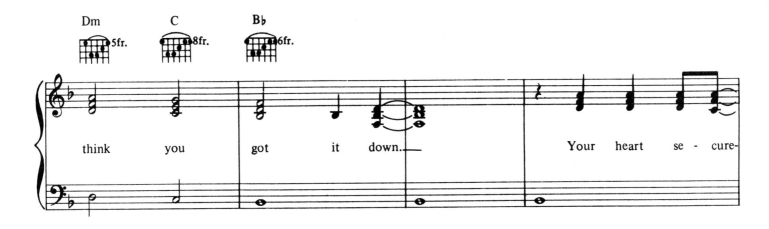

think you got it down.____ Your heart se - cure-

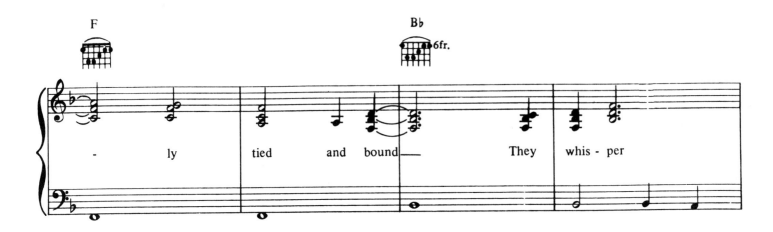

- ly tied and bound____ They whis - per

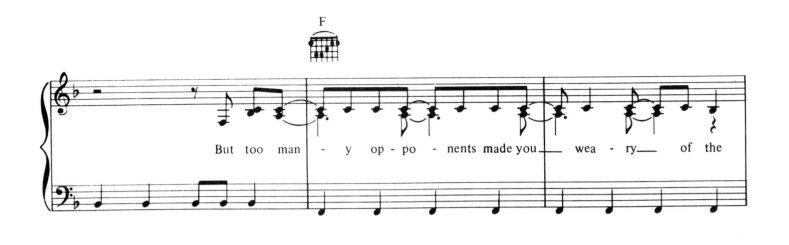

But too man - y op-po - nents made you____ wea-ry____ of the

fight.   Blind - ed by pas - sion, you

fool - ish - ly let some - one in.   All the

warn - ings went off in your head, still you had to give in.   Just when you

are both won and lost. On the edge is where it seems it's well worth the cost. Just when you think you got it down. Your heart in pieces on the ground

MORE SENSATIONAL MUSIC EXCLUSIVELY FROM CHERRY LANE

GREAT PIANO/VOCAL FOLIOS

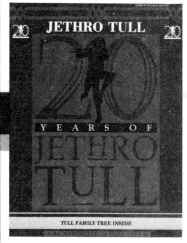

THE PAT BENATAR ANTHOLOGY
The best from one of the most electrifying female performers! Includes 34 songs from Benatar's smash albums IN THE HEAT OF THE NIGHT, CRIMES OF PASSION, PRECIOUS TIME, GET NERVOUS and LIVE FROM EARTH. Plus photos, feature articles and piano/vocal arrangements with guitar licks in standard and tablature notation.
CL#27619

WIDE AWAKE IN DREAMLAND
Pat Benatar is back in supreme form! The matching folio to her latest album which includes the hit single "All Fired Up," along with other songs such as "Don't Walk Away" and "One Love." Plus complete lyrics and a full color fold-out.
CL#27684

EVERYTHING
Climie Fisher
The debut album by the hot duo Climie Fisher. Includes the hits "Love Changes (Everything)" and "Rise to the Occasion."
CL#27685

20 YEARS OF JETHRO TULL
This definitive collection spans the twenty-year career of the mega-talented group, Jethro Tull. Songs include "Songs from the Wood," "Aqualung," "Love Story," plus a family tree full color fold-out.
CL#27682

Guitar Folios In Cherry Lane's exclusive PLAY-IT-LIKE-IT-IS Series

BILLY IDOL SONGBOOK
The hottest songs from Idol's first three albums including "Mony, Mony," "Hot in the City," and "Rebel Yell." Plus biography and outrageous photos.
CL#27620

WHIPLASH SMILE
Billy Idol
The matching folio to the best-selling album includes the songs "To Be A Lover," "Don't Need A Gun" and "Sweet Sixteen." Plus a sensational color fold-out.
CL#27659

PERFECT TIMING
MSG
Guitar legend Michael Schenker joins forces with former Grand Prix vocalist Robin McAuley in such great songs as "Gimme Your Love," "Love is Not a Game" and "No Time For Lovers." An authorized edition by <u>Guitar for the Practicing Musician</u> magazine.
CL#27671

VINNIE VINCENT INVASION
A collection of the meanest metal tunes from the albums VINNIE VINCENT INVASION and ALL SYSTEMS GO. Nine songs from the ex-Kiss band member include *Ashes to Ashes* and *Love Kills*. Plus a full color fold-out. An authorized edition by <u>Guitar for the Practicing Musician</u> magazine.
CL#27660

Catalogues are available upon request, please write to
CHERRY LANE MUSIC COMPANY, INC.
P.O. Box 430
Dept. BA
Port Chester, NY 10573

Cherry Lane Music Company, Inc.
"quality in printed music"
P.O. Box 430, Port Chester, NY 10573-430